CW00550775

HASTINGS TO

ASHFORD

and the New Romney branch

Vic Mitchell and Keith Smith

First published March 1987
Revised and reprinted October 1989
Reprinted April 1998

ISBN 0 906520 37 1

Design - Deborah Goodridge

Published by
     Middleton Press
     Easebourne Lane
     Midhurst, West Sussex
     GU29 9AZ
Tel: 01730 813169
Fax: 01730 812601

Printed & bound by Biddles Ltd,
     Guildford and Kings Lynn

CONTENTS

ACKNOWLEDGEMENTS

In addition to the many photographers credited in the captions, we are grateful to the following for assistance received – K. Catchpole, I. Dean, J. Drew, Mrs. E. Fisk, Dr. T. Gough, F. Laing, R. Randell, J. Snell, N. Stanyon and our ever helpful wives. Tickets are from the collections of G. Croughton and N. Langridge.

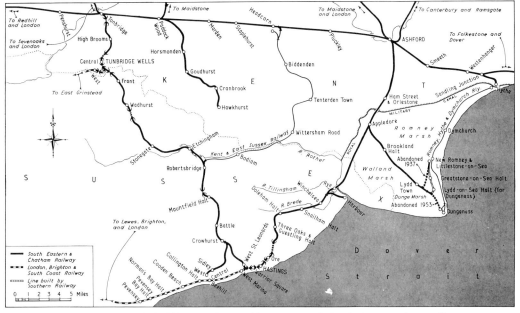

Railways between Ashford and Hastings, and associated lines, as at nationalisation, showing pre-grouping ownerships

(Railway Magazine)

GEOGRAPHICAL SETTING

Hastings is at the seaward end of the Wealden sandstone mass known as the Hastings Beds, which stretch west to Horsham. Their northern ridge is pierced by two tunnels beyond which the line descends steeply into the valley of the River Brede. The route traverses the Brede Levels and then crosses the River Tillingham just west of Rye and the River Rother a little to the east of it. The track continues almost level across the western edge of Walland Marsh and Romney Marsh before climbing onto Wealden Clay near Ham Street.

The middle third of the route is roughly parallel to the Royal Military Canal, which was redundant by the time it was completed in 1806, owing to Nelson's victory at Trafalgar. North of Rye the line is close to the Military Road, now part of the A259.

The importance of the coastal towns was recognised in 1278 when a Charter was granted to the Cinque Ports of Hastings, Romney, Hythe, Dover and Sandwich. Despite making a nonsense of the title, Winchelsea and Rye were added later, although the sea steadily receded from the latter two, and also from Romney.

Nowhere has the deposition of sea-borne material been more dramatic than at Dungeness where tons of flints, taken by the sea from cliffs further west, are added to the foreshore every year, having been rounded and polished en route. Thus the New Romney branch required virtually no civil engineering and certainly no imported ballast.

The last part of the route is on fairly level ground, over 100ft. above sea level. Ashford is situated at the confluence of the two parts of the River Stour, which flows north through Canterbury.

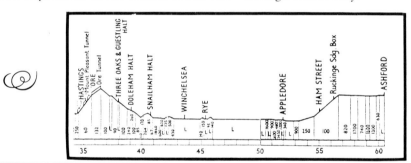

HISTORICAL BACKGROUND

The wide beaches of Dungeness have always been a perfect landing stage inviting enemy forces to enter the country by the easy route. Hence, when Parliament was considering plans for railways to Hastings, it opted for a line from Ashford as it would be strategically advantageous as a means of protecting the "open door". The South Eastern Railway thus had to accept that it was not likely to be a profitable route once more direct lines came into use.

The SER had reached Ashford from London in December 1842 but it was not until 13th February 1851 that its branch to Hastings was brought into use. Its more direct line via Tunbridge Wells was opened on 1st February 1852. The London, Brighton and South Coast Railway had reached the outskirts of St. Leonards in 1846 and Parliament decreed that it was to share its rival's station in Hastings. The feud and resulting farce is described in this section of our *Eastbourne to Hastings* album.

A single line branch from Appledore to Lydd was opened on 7th December 1881 and was extended to Dungeness for goods that day and for passengers on 1st April 1883. It was part of a grand scheme to provide an alternative route between London and Paris, which involved a direct rail link between Appledore, Tenterden and Headcorn. A harbour was to be excavated on Dungeness,

PASSENGER SERVICES

For most of the nineteenth century, the route was served by only four trains each way on weekdays, with two on Sundays. Soon after the introduction of the motor train services between Hastings and Rye in 1907, the number of through trains had increased to seven, with three on Sundays. Until the 1950s, the motor trains made four or five trips on weekdays, with one extended to Appledore for a period.

A regular interval service was ready for the 1959 season, with departures hourly and extra journeys at peak times. This service was modified and reduced in May 1979, in preparation for single line working between Ore and Appledore, and it is still basically on an hourly interval.

Through working has been limited, but one of the benefits of the amalgamation of the railway companies in 1923 was the introduction, by the Southern Railway in 1924, of some through services between Brighton and the Kent Coast. Destinations included Margate, Folkestone and Dover. These were withdrawn upon the electrification of the Brighton to Hastings route in 1935, despite great public outcry. If the Southern electrification is eventually completed, maybe the various operating departments could be persuaded to co-operate and run a Dover-Weymouth service, now that through trains for passenger convenience are back in fashion. Network South Coast could serve nearly a million people!

New Romney Branch

The weekday service increased from six to ten trains per day up to WWII, with a Sunday service being provided during most of the summers. Some journeys were to Dungeness only; some to New Romney only and some to both, involving reversal at Lydd. A detailed chronicle would be complicated and tedious. Most trains ran through to Ashford although a few terminated at Appledore.

Services were not curtailed during WWII, owing to the very large military presence in the area. When the holiday trade was revived after the war there were some extra journeys on Saturdays, including through steam trains to and from London. Diesel locomotives preceded the introduction of diesel-electric multiple units (DEMUs), which provided a service of two-hour intervals up to the closure.

the entrance to it being on the leeward side. The excavated material was to be sold as building ballast in London but, like the grandiose Manchester & Milford Haven Railway, little was achieved. Eventually, a 3-mile branch was opened from the main branch to New Romney on 19th June 1884.

The next milestone in the railway history of the district was the opening of the 15″ gauge Romney, Hythe & Dymchurch Railway between those places (but not in that order!) on 16th July 1927. It was extended further south along the coast to Dungeness in August 1928. Holiday camps and homes were being built in the area in the early 1930s and so the Southern Railway decided to divert its New Romney branch to a route nearer the coast and cease passenger services to the Dungeness terminus. This it did on 4th July 1937, the remains of the Dungeness branch being lifted in 1952-53.

Passenger services were withdrawn from the New Romney branch on 6th March 1967 but part of the line remains in use for the transport of waste from the Dungeness Nuclear Power Stations.

In 1970 the Hastings-Ashford passenger services were expected to be withdrawn but they were given a two-year reprieve, pending road improvements. Eventually economies were effected by automating most of the level crossings and, in 1979, the double track was singled between Ore and Appledore, using a tokenless block safety system.

HASTINGS

1. The earliest view we have of the station shows a passenger train standing at the through platform, with the roof of the engine shed in the background. The row of "chimneys" housed the oil lights and the wagon carried the horse drawn coach of a wealthy passenger. It would be shunted to an end-loading dock for removal. (Hastings Library)

The 1929 map shows the layout that prevailed until the major rebuild in 1931. Only one platform was provided for through trains whilst three terminal platforms were available for trains arriving from the west. This was a legacy from the days when the SER was obliged to provide a bay for the LBSCR; later two more platforms were added, mainly for use in the summer.

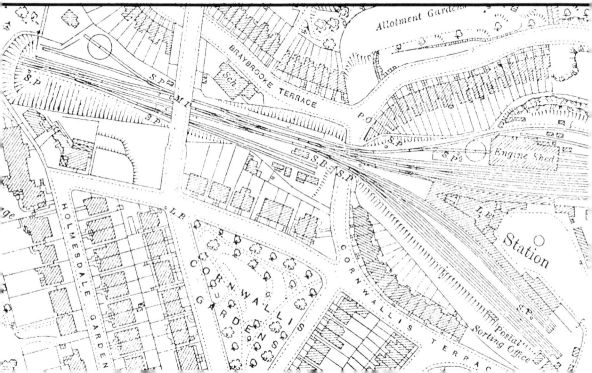

2. For many years the railmotor service between Hastings and Rye was operated by a composite engine and coach, seen here trailing another coach. The railcar was one of eight built by Kitson & Co in 1906. The East Box can be seen standing astride the first of eight sidings. Beyond the South Terrace bridge, a siding was provided to the gas works. (D. Cullum collection)

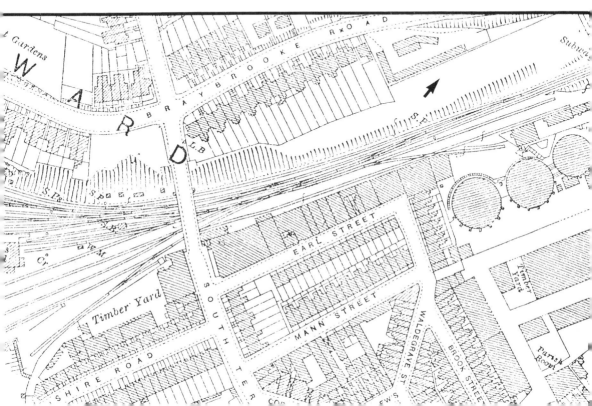

3. This 1950 view shows that the station was rebuilt with two island platforms, which gave much greater flexibility. Prior to WWII, the station staff numbered 170 to 200, from winter to summer, which was greater than the total population of Winchelsea. Two of the sidings are spanned by a gantry crane of 10-ton capacity. (D. Clayton)

4. After the withdrawal of the unsuccessful railmotors, the stopping service to Rye was hauled by various tank engines. This example is ex-LBSCR class D3 no. 2378, seen bearing the prefix S, shortly after nationalisation. Its tank is overflowing whilst the locomotive is filled from the other side, there being a balancing pipe under the boiler. (J.J. Smith)

5. Relief trains from London often ran via Ashford. This example is composed of former LSWR coaches behind "Schools" class no. 30936 *Cranleigh*, on 26th May 1950. Down trains arrive from both directions at Hastings and change their description when passing through the station. (S.C. Nash)

6. Electrification of services from East-bourne took place on 7th July 1935 and they were extended to Ore as inadequate carriage sidings could be provided at Hastings. Here witness the arrival of a Victoria-bound train on 28th August 1985, after lay-over at Ore, a practice which largely ceased in May 1986, when Ore shed closed. (J. Scrace)

7. Platform 1 has been used primarily for Ashford trains for many years and hence the west end of the platform has been little used. Early in 1986, the track was lifted from that part and a covered footway constructed which enables passengers to gain direct access to the booking hall, on the level. (V. Mitchell)

8. The railway from Ore originally approached Hastings station entirely on an embankment, built in the fields of Priory Farm. It was pierced by a small tunnel, 120ft long, through which passed Ore Lane, the forerunner of Queens Road. In 1898, this bottleneck to the town's traffic was eliminated by the construction of a bridge on tall fluted iron columns. Here we see the main lines interlaced to give more space for the civil engineers to work. Interlacing was a common practice on tramways in narrow streets. (Hastings Library)

9. The new bridge gave ample clearance for tram cars, the first one running in the town in 1905. These were superseded by trolleybuses in 1927, some of which were single deckers, uncommon in Britain. (Hastings Library)

ORE

10. The other intermediate stations on the route were brought into use when the line opened. Ore station opened its doors on 1st January 1888 to serve a developing residential area. Points of interest in this deteriorated print are the SER signal, with white circle and remote spectacles, and the footbridge at the east end. (Lens of Sutton)

← 11. Mount Pleasant Tunnel is 230yds long and was anything but pleasant for eastbound locomotive crews climbing the 1 in 60 gradient, although there is one air shaft. The down platform now has a glass waiting shelter and the up platform has lost its canopy. (Lens of Sutton)

12. D class 4–4–0 no. 1549 emerges from its own smoke on 26th June 1946, with the 10.08 am Hastings to Ashford service. The roof of the 1935 shed for electric stock is on the right. (D. Cullum collection)

SOUTHERN RAILWAY.
This ticket is not transferable and is issued subject to the Company's Bye-laws, Regulations and Conditions in their Time Tables, Notices and Book of Regulations.
Ore to
Ore   Ore
Hastings   Hastings
HASTINGS
THIRD CLASS   THIRD CLASS
Fare 2d.   Fare 2d.
1596   1596

SOUTHERN RAILWAY.
Issued subject to the Bye-laws, Regulations & Conditions in the Company's Bills and Notices.
Ore to
Ore   Ore
Doleham Halt   Doleham Halt
DOLEHAM HALT
THIRD CLASS   THIRD CLASS
Fare 10½d.   Fare 10½d.
NOT TRANSFERABLE.
3744   3744

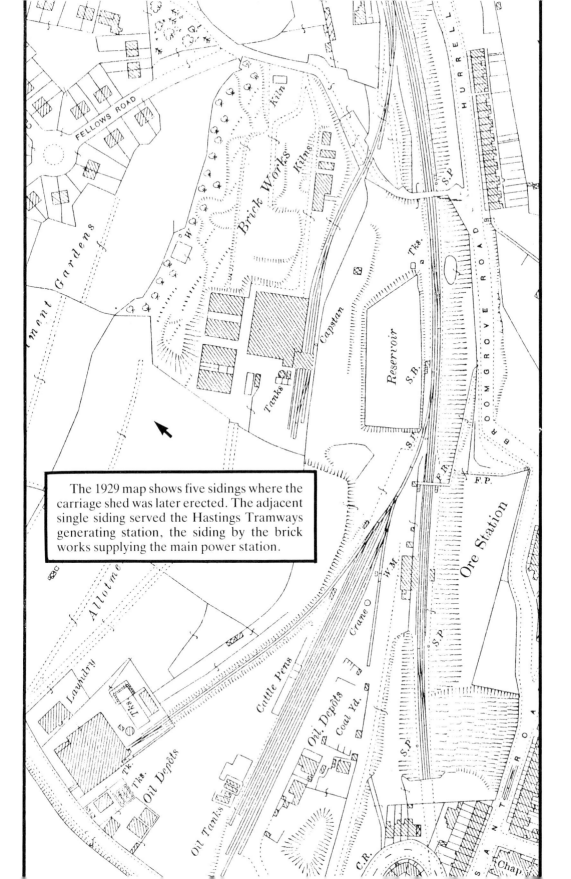

The 1929 map shows five sidings where the carriage shed was later erected. The adjacent single siding served the Hastings Tramways generating station, the siding by the brick works supplying the main power station.

13. The former Hastings Tramways siding is visible beyond the cab of this grimy K class, photographed in the up platform on 7th February 1961. Above its tender, the products of the carriage cleaners smoulder gently. (P. Pannett)

14. Most railway companies preferred sliding windows on their signal boxes, rather than the sash style seen here in September 1969. Its functions have been undertaken from Hastings box since 30th January 1977. (J. Scrace)

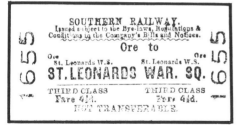

SOUTHERN RAILWAY.
Issued subject to the Bye-laws, Regulations & Conditions in the Company's Bills and Notices.
Ore to
Ore St. Leonards W.S.   Ore St. Leonards W.S.
ST. LEONARDS WAR. SQ.
THIRD CLASS   THIRD CLASS
Fare 4½d.   Fare 4½d.
NOT TRANSFERABLE.

◀────── 15. The 11.28 to Victoria reverses towards the electrified headshunt which extends as far as the mouth of Ore Tunnel. A London train entered the carriage shed every hour, and 27 minutes were allowed for it to be swept through. The date is 6th September 1969. (J. Scrace)

◀──────
16. In 1987, the station was repainted with olive frames, white sashes and stone boards. The gradient of the track is evident when looking at the brick base of the timber building. By this time, Victoria trains used the headcode 72. (V. Mitchell)

17. The carriage shed had four roads and before the withdrawal of freight services there were a further six before reaching the "Tramways" siding. The electrified one nearest the shed was retained, as can be seen in this view from the 16.44 from Ashford on 30th July 1985. The up service waits at 17.30 to enter the single line to Rye. (V. Mitchell)

18. Part of the brickworks, shown on the map, is visible in the top left corner of this photograph of the Ashford to Hastings goods, taken on 16th November 1960. The Q1 is passing Ore down home and above its cab is the gate on the private siding to the Power Station. Look for the shadow of the old style bridge weight restriction sign. (P. Pannett).

20. 25 years later and 25 yards north we see the disused Power Station line and the facing crossover added in 1979 to enable up trains to cross to the former down line which forms the single track to Rye, nearly 10 miles distant. The electrified up line was retained for terminating trains only. (V. Mitchell)

1890

LONDON, ASHFORD, LYDD, NEW ROMNEY, DUNGENESS, and HASTINGS.—South Eastern.						
DOWN.	mrn mrn mrn aft aft aft	aft aft aft aft	mrn aft
90 CHARING CROSS dp	5 40 8 10 8 43 1030 11 6 1215	4 30 ... 7 8	7 45 6 26
90 CANNON STREET dp	5 50 8 20 8 45 1042 11 5 1227	4 40 ... 7 8	7 55 6 30
90 LONDON BRIDGE "	5 55 8 25 — 1047 — 12 0	4 43 ... 7 13	7 53 6 33
Ashford dep	8 45 1044 1 0 ... 3 5	6 15 ... 8 52	1045 9 0
Ham Street	8 55 1053 1 10 — 3 15	6 25 ... 9 3	1055 9 10
Appledore arr	9 2 11 0 1 17 ... 3 25	6 32 ... 9 10	11 29 9 17
Appledore dep 8 ... 11 5 ... 1 20 ... 3 27	1 25 6 35 7 50		
Brookland 8 10 ... 1112 ... 1 25 ... 3 31	1 30 6 40 7 55		
Lydd arr 8 20 ... 1122 aft 1 35 afc 3 41	4 39 6 50 8 5		
Lydd dep 8 21 ... 1123 1255 1 36 2 40 3 42	4 46 6 51 8 6		
New Romney* ar 8 28 ... 1132 1257 1 45 2 50 3 52	4 50 7 0 8 15		
Lydd dep ... ... 1150 ... 2 5 ...	5 18 ... 8 35		
Dungeness arr ... ... 12 0 ... 2 15 ...	5 28 ... 8 45		
Rye	9 16 1114 ... 1 31 ... 3 36	6 46 ... 9 24	1118 9 31
Winchelsea	9 23 1121 ... 1 38 ... 3 43	6 53 ... 9 31	1129 9 37
Ore	9 40 1140 ... 1 55 ... 4 0	7 10 ... 9 48	1140 9 54
Hastings 93, 74 arr	9 48 1146 ... 2 3 ... 4 8	7 18 ... 9 56	1148 10 2

Up.	mrn mrn mrn aft aft aft	aft aft aft aft	mrn aft
Hastings dep	7 15 9 15 ... 1 5	3 40 ... 7 5	7 0 5 45
Ore	7 19 9 19 ... 1 9	3 44 ... 7 9	7 4 5 49
Winchelsea	7 36 9 36 ... 1 26	4 1 ... 7 26	7 21 6 6
Rye	7 42 9 42 ... 1 31	4 7 ... 7 32	7 27 6 12
Dungeness dep 6 50 ... ... 1210 ... ... 2 28 ... 5 58			
Lydd arr 6 59 ... ... 1220 ... ... 2 35 ... 6 8			
New Romney*dp 7 25 9 20 1135 ... 1245 1 50 2955 3 57 5 57 10 8 20			
Lydd arr 7 34 9 29 1145 ... 1254 2 0 3 5 4 4 5 5 13 7 19 8 30			
Lydd dep 7 35 9 30 ... ... 1255 ... 3 5 5 4 6 6 10 7 20			
Brookland 7 45 9 40 ... ... 1 5 ... 3 15 5 14 1 6 20 7 30			
Appledore arr 7 50 9 45 ... ... 1 10 ... 3 20 5 18 6 25 7 35			
Appledore dep 7 57 9 57 ... ... 1 47 ... 4 2 ... 7 47 7 426 27			
Ham Street 8 5 10 5 ... ... 1 55 ... 4 30 ... 7 55 7 506 35			
Ashford 93, 90 arr 8 18 1018 ... 2 8 ... 4 43 ... 8 8 8 8 36 48			
93 LONDON BRIDGE af 1039 1147 ... 4 9 ... 7 15 ... 1018 1025 9 10			
93 CANNON STREET " 1044 1152 ... 4 14 ... 7 25 ... 1023 1029 9 14			
93 CHARING CROSS " 1055 12 5 ... 4 27 ... 7 35 ... 1035 1042 9 27			

19. "Schools" class *Bradfield* climbs the 1 in 60 gradient towards Ore Tunnel, through which the incline eases to 1 in 132. The level crossing gates on the Power Station siding are visible in this 1961 view. Note their unusual white diamond targets. (S.C. Nash)

21. The Hastings Corporation Electricity Works was inherited by the Central Electricity Generating Board and produced 13.8MW, latterly only at peak times. Up to five wagons could be pushed up to the works and some were unloaded into the stock yard, on the left. This involved much laborious shovelling. (P. Pannett)

22. The immediate coal requirements for the station were tipped direct into the hopper and the wagons were shunted by rope and capstan, as seen here. The boilers were converted to oil firing in the mid-1960s and the works were demolished in the early 1970s. (P. Pannett)

23. The wagons were mostly wooden-bodied and had to be chained to the tippler before emptying. The present gas turbine station is 120MW capacity and is fuelled by oil. (P. Pannett)

2nd - SINGLE		SINGLE - 2nd
8	Ore to	8
3	Ore Three Oaks and Guestling Halt	Ore Three Oaks and Guestling Halt	3
0	**THREE OAKS &**	0
0	**GUESTLING HALT**	0
0	(S) 9d. Fare 9d. (S)	0
	For conditions see over For conditions see over	

THREE OAKS

24. Ore tunnel is 1042yds long and, like the other tunnels near Hastings, presented serious problems during construction due to beds of rock, clay and water bearing strata being encountered. Major maintenance work in 1953-54, necessitated single line working, which involved temporary provision of crossovers and a signal box 500yds north of the tunnel. H class no. 31295 propels the 2.10pm Appledore to Hastings motor train, past the two Ore down distant signals on 2nd October 1954. (J.J. Smith)

25. Looking north, we see the signal box in the distance and its two up home signals. Provision was made for either track to be used by passenger trains while the Engineer occupied the other. The skips seen in the previous photograph were lifted by the road crane seen here. (J.J. Smith)

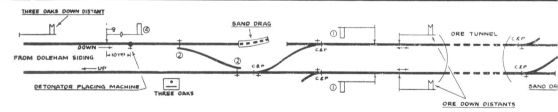

26. The signal box had the customary coal bunker, rainwater tank and fire buckets. The crossing timbers eased the path of the signal- man when handing the tablet (from the Tyler's No. 6 instrument) to passing train crews. (J.J. Smith)

27. This halt, and the following two, were opened for the motor train service on 1st July 1907. Originally Three Oaks Bridge, the "Bridge" was soon dropped as it only referred to the nearby road bridge. The suffix "& Guestling" was added and eventually both this and "Halt" were dropped. Only the former down platform, on the left, remains in use today, serving a scattered community. (Lens of Sutton)

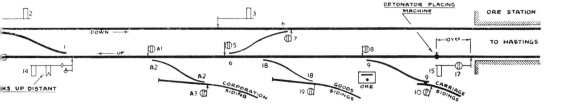

THREE OAKS, (Nº SHOWN THUS :-④)

DOWN RUNNING SIGNAL.
4. DOWN HOME.

UP RUNNING SIGNALS.
1. UP HOMES.

ORE

DOWN RUNNING SIGNALS.
2. DOWN OUTER HOME.
3. DOWN INNER HOME.

UP RUNNING SIGNALS.
14. UP ADVANCED STARTING.
15. UP STARTING.
17. NEW SHUNTING SIGNAL.

DOLEHAM

28. Opened as Guestling, the name was soon altered to that of a nearby farm, as Three Oaks was closer to most of Guestling. Upon singling only the concrete up platform on the right was retained. (D. Cullum)

29. Normally one DEMU is sufficient but in April 1981 the formation is seen doubled as a Hampshire set leads an Oxted set towards Hastings. No platform lights exist and so locating lamps are provided – one is seen on the right of the previous picture.
(J.A.M. Vaughan)

30. In 1899, Hastings Corporation commenced construction of a waterworks 1½ miles north west of the halt, near the village of Brede. This 18″ gauge saddle tank was supplied by Bagnalls for the work and after the pumps started in 1904 it was used to haul coal from a quay on the River Brede, using four 4-ton wooden bogie wagons. In about 1920, barges were abandoned in favour of a Sentinel Steam Waggon, working from Doleham siding. The railway closed in 1935, when coal was transported entirely by road. (Hastings Library)

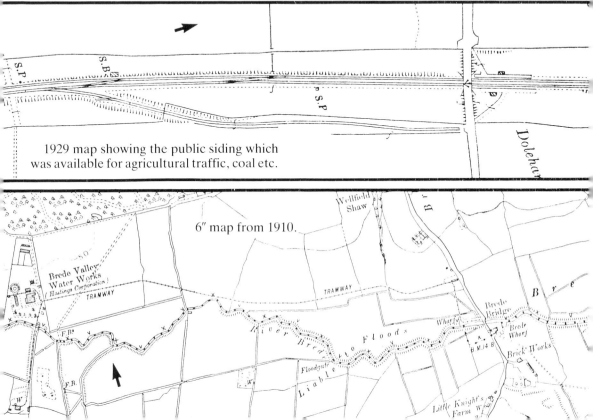

1929 map showing the public siding which was available for agricultural traffic, coal etc.

6″ map from 1910.

SNAILHAM HALT

31. This remote structure was nearly ½ mile from the nearest dwelling and was approached along an unsurfaced lane. This is the view towards Brede Levels and Winchelsea, before services were withdrawn in 1959. Whistle boards were provided 250 yds either side of the level crossing which is partly visible in the foreground. (Lens of Sutton)

32. The main buildings were adjacent to the down platform and therefore closer to the town. This is more than ½ mile to the south and has a more interesting history than the station. It was totally destroyed by a storm in 1287 and was partly rebuilt to a geometric pattern on a nearby hump of higher land. It is thus one of the earliest examples of New Town planning. (Lens of Sutton)

33. The SER had staggered platforms at most of their stations on the assumption that it was safer for passengers to cross the lines behind a departing train. This was fine until traffic increased significantly on the other line – it never did at Winchelsea.
(Lens of Sutton)

2nd-PRIVILEGE
RETURN

Rye
(5664) to
WINCHELSEA
HALT
(S)   Fare 0/4
For conditions see over

PRIVILEGE-2nd
RETURN

Winchelsea
Halt
to   (5664)
RYE
Fare 0/4   (S)
For conditions see over

1319

1313

WINCHELSEA

Down — Week Days

Miles from Ashford	Station	a.m.	a.m.	a.m.	a.m.	a.m.	a.m.	a.m. 8O	a.m. SX	a.m.	a.m.	a.m. 8O	a.m.	p.m.	p.m.	p.m.	p.m. 8O	p.m. 8O	p.m. 8X	p.m.	p.m.
	20 Charing Cross .... dep	..	..	7B11	..	7B11	9 15	..	..	9 15	11½	11½	..	1 55	..	1 15	..	2 15	..	3 15	..	..
	20 Waterloo .... "	..	7 0 M	7B13	..	7B13	9 17	..	..	9 17	11½	11½	..	..	..	1 17	..	..	..	3 17	..	..
	20 Cannon Street .... "	..	5B13	..	7 23	7B24	..	..	..	..	..	..	..	150½	..	..	..	..	..	..	..	..
	20 London Bridge .... "	3B40	5B13	..	7 23	7B27	..	..	..	..	..	..	12 2	..	..	..	..	..	..	..	..	..
	20 Victoria .... "	..	..	..	7 18	..	..	..	..	9 13	..	11½	..	..	..	..	..	..	..	..	..	..
—	Ashford (Kent) .... dep	5 45	8 0	9 12	..	9 48	..	..	10¼	..	11 55	12 53	1 12	1 33	..	..	2 52	..	3 35	4 34	4 44	4 55
5½	Ham Street and Orlestone	5 53	8 8	9 20	..	9 58	..	..	10 56	..	..	1 1	1 20	..	..	3 0	..	3 43	4 42	4 52	..
8½	Appledore	5 59	8 14	9 26	..	10 4	..	..	11 4	..	..	1 1	1 26	1 47	55	3 6	..	3 49	4 48	4 57	5 6
—	Appledore .... dep	6 0	8 21	..	..	10 10	..	11 24	..	..	1 9	..	1 43	..	..	3 50	5	10 4	54	..	..
11	Brookland	6 6	8 26	..	..	10 15	..	11 31	..	..	1 15	..	1 55	..	..	3 57	5	17 5	4	..	..
15½	Lydd Town	6 18	8 35	..	..	10 24	..	11 40	..	..	1 24	..	2 4	..	..	4	6 5	28 5	13	..	..
18½	Lydd-on-Sea H	6 37	8 43	..	..	10 31	..	11 49	..	..	1 32	..	2 13	..	..	4	15 5	36 5	23	..	..
20½	Greatstone-on-Sea	6 42	8 48	..	..	10 35	..	11 54	..	..	1 37	..	2 19	..	..	4 20	5	41 5	27	..	..
22	New Romney L .... arr	6 46	8 52	..	..	10 39	..	11 58	..	..	1 41	..	2 23	..	..	4 27	5	45 5	31	..	..
15½	Rye	..	8 27	9 37	9 50	..	10 15	11 15	..	12 16	..	..	1 38	..	2 6	3 17	4	..	..	5 1	6 8
17½	Winchelsea	..	8 33	..	9 54	..	..	11 21	..	..	..	..	..	..	2 11	3 22	4 12	..	..	5 2	6 12
19½	Snailham Halt	..	..	..	10 0	..	..	11 26	..	..	..	..	..	..	2 17	..	4 18	..	..	..	6 18
21½	Doleham Halt .... [Halt]	..	8 41	..	10 5	..	..	11 31	..	..	..	..	..	..	2 22	..	4 22	..	..	..	6 23
22½	Three Oaks and Guestling	..	8 45	..	10 10	..	..	11 37	..	..	..	..	..	..	2 27	..	4 27	..	..	..	6 28
25½	Ore	..	8 51	9 53	10 16	..	..	11 45	..	..	12 35	..	1 54	..	2 34	..	4 34	..	..	5 5	6 36
26½	Hastings .... arr	..	8 55	9 57	10 20	..	10 31	11 49	..	..	12 39	..	1 58	..	2 38	3 38	4 38	..	..	5 10	6 40

Down — Week Days — continued

Station	p.m. 8X	p.m. 8O	p.m.	p.m.	p.m.	p.m.	p.m.	p.m.	a.m.	a.m.	a.m.	a.m.	a.m.	a.m.	a.m.	p.m.	p.m.	p.m.	p.m.	p.m.	p.m.
20 Charing Cross .... dep	4 34	..	4SO34	5Y30	..	7 34	7 15	..	..	9 36	..	11 10	..	12 15	..	3 15	..	..	8 10		
20 Waterloo .... "	4 36	..	4SO36	5Y32	..	7 37	7 17	..	..	9 39	..	11 13	..	12 17	..	3 17	..	..	8 13		
20 Cannon Street .... "	5 0	..	4 42	6SX32	..	7 24	..	..	9 45	..	..	..	..	..							
20 London Bridge .... "	..	4 47	4SX35	6SO33	6SO18	7 26	..	7 15	..	9 45	..	11 20	..	..	3 23	..	..	8 21			
20 Victoria .... "	4 18	..	..	..	..	7 20	..	9 18	..	..	..	11 18	..	5 18							
Ashford (Kent) .... dep	6 12	6 28	7 8	7 52	8 59	9 42	9 18	..	11 30	11 50	12 10	2 15	..	4 55	..	7 15	..	9 50			
Ham Street and Orlestone	6 20	6 36	3 0	..	9 50	9 28	..	11 38	11 58	1 18	..	2 36	..	7 23	..	9 58					
Appledore	6 26	6 42	7 20	3 6	9 58	9 31	9 59	11 43	12 4	1 24	2 38	..	5 6	7 28	..	10 4					
Appledore .... dep	6 34	6 48	..	8 12	..	10 10	9 32	..	11 44	..	2 27	..	5 7								
Brookland	6 39	6 53	..	8 17	..	10 15	9 41	..	11 53	..	2 36	5 16	..								
Lydd Town	6 48	7 2	..	8 26	..	10 28	9 50	..	12 2	..	2 45	5 25	..								
Lydd-on-Sea H	6 55	7 9	..	8 33	..	10 35	9 57	..	12 9	..	2 52	5 32	..								
Greatstone-on-Sea	7 0	7 14	..	8 41	..	10 40	10 2	..	12 14	..	2 57	5 37	..								
New Romney L .... arr	7 4	7 18	..	8 45	..	10 44	10 6	..	12 19	..	3 1	5 41	..								
Rye	6 39	6 53	7 31	8 17	9 19	10 11	..	9 39	..	10 11	11 25	..	12 16	1 36	2 20	5 0	..	6 39	41	9 10	10 17
Winchelsea	..	..	..	8 22	..	10 16	..	9 43	..	11 29	..	12 21	..	2 24	5 4	..	6 43	47	9 14	10 22	
Snailham Halt	..	..	..	..	..	..	9 48	..	11 34	..	..	2 29	5 9	..	6 48	..	9 19				
Doleham Halt .... [Halt]	..	..	..	..	..	Bb	..	9 52	..	11 38	..	..	2 33	5 13	..	6 52	..	9 23			
Three Oaks and Guestling	..	..	..	..	..	..	9 57	..	11 43	..	..	2 38	5 18	..	6 57	..	9 28				
Ore	..	..	7 47	8 36	9 36	10 33	10 5	10 27	11 51	..	12 36	..	2 46	5 26	..	7 5	3	9 36	10 37		
Hastings .... arr	..	..	7 51	8 40	9 40	10 37	10 10	10 31	11 56	..	12 40	1 55	2 51	5 30	..	7 10	4	9 41	10 42		

And the Sundays columns follow to the right of the continued table.

‡ 1 min. later on Saturdays
B Third class only
Bb Stops to set down on informing the Guard at the previous stopping station
H For Dungeness
L New Romney & Littlestone-on-Sea
8O or SO Saturdays only
8X or SX Saturdays excepted
Y Dep. Charing Cross 6 15 and Waterloo 6 17 p.m. on Saturdays

34. N class no. 31405 retards its loose coupled wagons on 4th June 1958, as the decorators start to smarten up the building. There was no EXIT sign, but at least the gentlemen knew where to go. (J.H. Aston)

35. It is evident that by 1969 the signal box, siding and foot crossing had gone but the crossing keeper was retained and provided with signals on each line. (E. Wilmshurst)

37. After the New Town was built the sea slowly receded from the port of Winchelsea, until now it is over a mile distant. History has repeated itself in that passengers have more quickly disappeared from the station but its elegant building still stands, albeit surrounded by an untidy muddle. (Lens of Sutton) ⟶

36. Further cut backs included the shelter's canopy and the crossing keeper. An automatic open crossing has been installed, which requires a speed limit for trains of 20 mph. (Lens of Sutton)

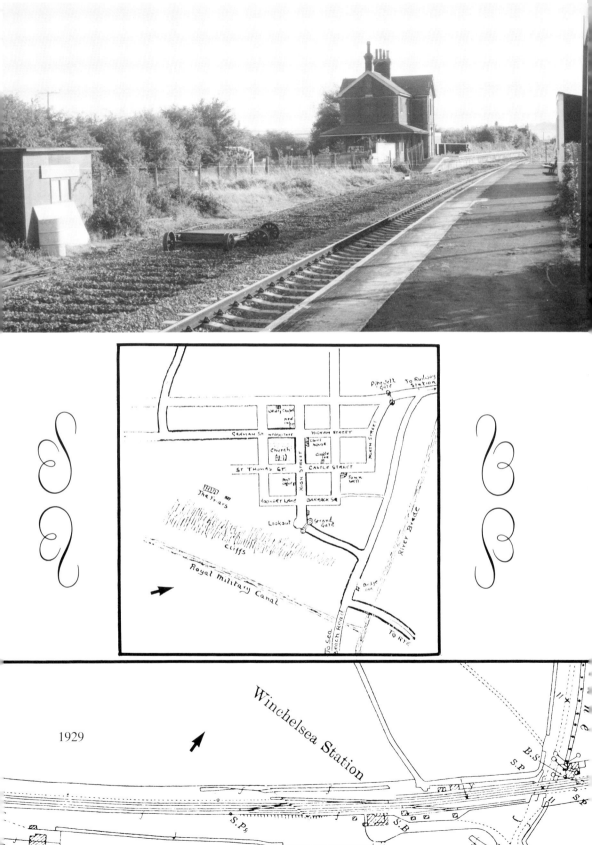

Winchelsea Station

RYE HARBOUR BRANCH

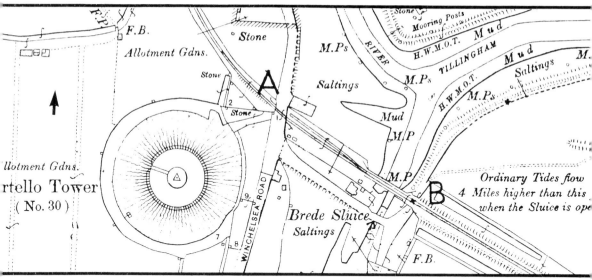

The SER was required by Parliament to make considerable and expensive improvements to Rye Harbour and so when the branch was opened in 1854 there was talk of using the new facilities for a ferry service to France but this never came about. The line branched off in a trailing direction when approached from Ashford and the first siding was located shortly after crossing the Winchelsea Road, as shown on this 1909 map. Later records show it as an oil company's siding. Next was John Carter's siding, on the same side of the line.

Further south, a trailing siding ran into the chemical works of South Eastern Tar Distilleries, across the public highway and into the other part of the works. Here it became dual gauge with the firm's internal narrow gauge system, right down to the waterfront. This is the 1909 edition, there being no works shown on the 1898 map. The narrow gauge lines crossed the road to a gigantic ground level tar vat. Standard gauge track can still be seen in one of the gateways, the site now being occupied by an oil refinery and firm that reprocesses solvents.

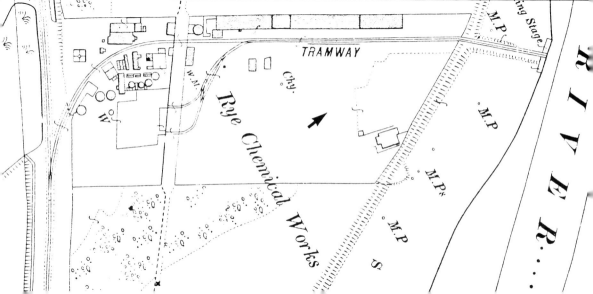

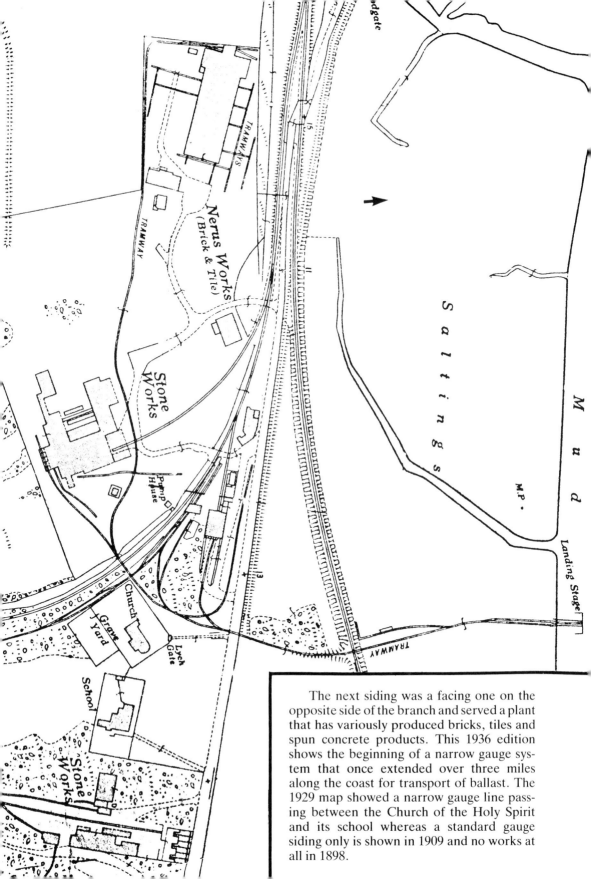

The next siding was a facing one on the opposite side of the branch and served a plant that has variously produced bricks, tiles and spun concrete products. This 1936 edition shows the beginning of a narrow gauge system that once extended over three miles along the coast for transport of ballast. The 1929 map showed a narrow gauge line passing between the Church of the Holy Spirit and its school whereas a standard gauge siding only is shown in 1909 and no works at all in 1898.

38. The final position of the railway pier is seen in the background and was in line with the end of the branch. The inn sign is that of the *William the Conqueror* mentioned on the map. (R.C. Riley)

In 1872 the branch ended with three wagon turntables, widely used at that time when a horse would often be used for shunting purposes. Tram Road exists today, on the route of the line to the Concrete Works.

6″ scale 1909

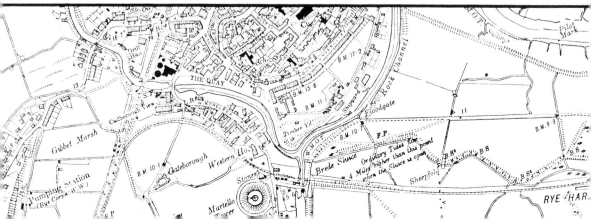

Rye Harbour
Coastguard Station

Flagstaff

William the Conquerer
(P H)

7¹

Post
Office

Tank   *Tank*

Tank

Tank

Flagstaff

Reading Rooms   Ship Inn

Prospect Cottage

Stone

Tank

Tank

R Y

H A R B

High Water Mark of Ordinary Tides

Tank

Concrete Works

Tank   *Stone*

River Rother

Mark of Ordinary

Salting

Pilot
Mark   Landing Stage   Pilot
Mark

F.B.

RYE & CAMBER TRAMWAY

Tank

S a l t i n   g

F.P.   F.B.

F. B.   F.B.

*Pilot
Mark*   Mud   Post

B S   Post

R I V E R   . . R O T H E R . .

Mud   Mooring Stages

Golf Link
Station

Signal

Mud

Salting   Post

Rye
Chemical Wks.

TRAMWAY

Pilot
Marks   Post

S a l t i n g s

*Pilot
Mark*

Ferry   RYE HARBOUR

Lighthouse
Fixed & W

B.M. 13

Floodgate

10

F.B

Coastguard
Station

P P

Watch
House

M P

B.M. 9 2

15

Msn.
Room

Church of the
Holy Spirit   School

C H   B.M. 16 9

Sewage Work

Scrugge
Pumping Sta

Vicarage

Harbour

W   D

Hard

39. By 1930, the pier at the end of the line had become unsafe and so new buffers were erected on firm ground. Presumably the old ones were too much part of the pier to be easily removed. This photograph taken on 21st September 1950 shows partially built shock absorbing vans, stored prior to completion at Ashford Works. (R.C. Riley)

40. The building on the left was the intermediate station of the Rye & Camber Tramway which ran on the opposite side of the River Rother, across which a ferry was provided for passengers. The 3ft gauge line closed in 1939 but the station still stands. The Rye Harbour branch closed on 29th January 1960 although it had been little used in its final years. (Lens of Sutton)

RYE

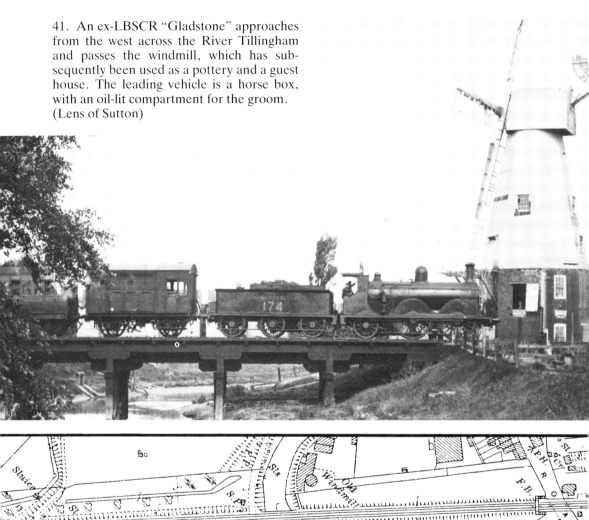

41. An ex-LBSCR "Gladstone" approaches from the west across the River Tillingham and passes the windmill, which has subsequently been used as a pottery and a guest house. The leading vehicle is a horse box, with an oil-lit compartment for the groom. (Lens of Sutton)

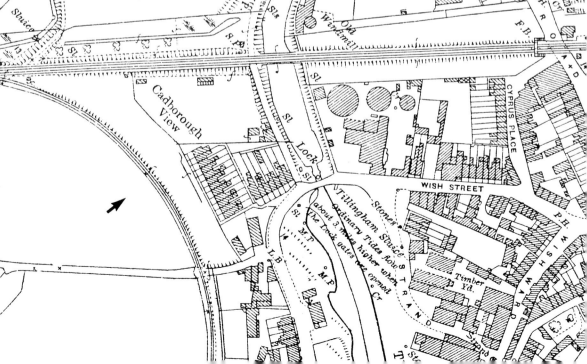

42. This view of the west end of the station is from the footbridge by Ferry Road level crossing. The box controlling its gates is on the right. A railcar is running past the spacious goods shed, which appears to be scaffolded for roof repairs. (Lens of Sutton)

The Harbour branch curves away on the left of this 1929 map, the proximity of the cattle market to the station being another interesting feature. The goods shed closed in 1963 and was demolished in 1984.

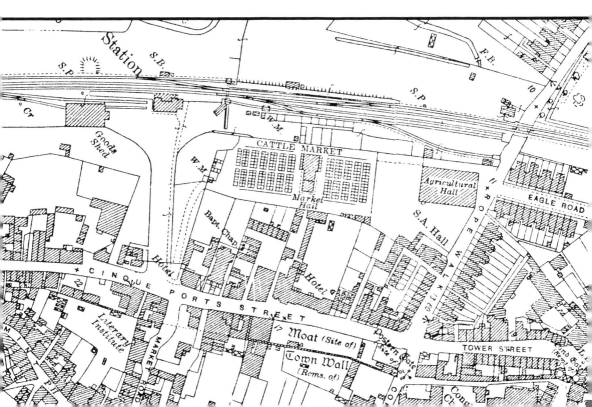

43. At under 30 tons, the SECR P class locomotive was an economical machine for lightly loaded rural lines. Examples are to be found preserved on the Bluebell and Kent & East Sussex Railways. (S.C. Nash collection)

OOOO

S. E. R.

Winchelsea to

RYE

First 7d

45. A through train from Ashford arrives behind no. A470, a former SECR D class 4–4–0, on 12th July 1931. The picture shows the location of the cattle pens, the double sided water column and that only gentlemen had facilities on the up platform. (H.C. Casserley)

44. Although over a third heavier, the LBSCR D1 design was widely used on local services after the formation of the SR. This example is no. B224 and is seen with the 6.10pm auto train for Hastings on 29th August 1931. (K. Nunn/LCGB)

46. The driver sits in the comfort of his cab whilst the fireman struggles to water the locomotive on his own. Railway features of interest are the wagon turntable, the wagon weighbridge (in the siding to the right of the boy's head), the water tower and the sighting board behind the arm of the up starting signal. (Lens of Sutton)

47. H class 0–4–4T no. 31520, another former SECR locomotive, waits to leave with the 2.53 pm Ashford to Hastings train on 4th June 1958. The first coach is match-board, a type once common in the area. (J.H. Aston)

48. As in the previous picture, the sidings are full. In the distance we see the gates of Ferry Road crossing which were replaced by lifting barriers, overseen by CCTV. The most unusual industrial item in the town is the oval brick-built public water cistern dating from 1735, which is located in the corner of the churchyard. (Lens of Sutton)

49. The 30-lever signal box from 1893 survived in 1987 and controlled the tokenless block section single line sections to Ore and Appledore. This 1967 view shows the rods and wires which were lost when colour light signals came into use on 1st October 1979. (J. Scrace)

The route crosses into Kent about three miles east of Rye but before doing so it passes over the River Rother. The early swing bridge was rebuilt in 1903 with fixed spans, which are shown under test in Picture no. 57 in *Steaming through East Sussex*.
(Middleton Press)

50. The route was included in Phase 2 of the Kent electrification scheme and some preliminary work was done in the early 1960s, before the plan was dropped. This included the erection of a footbridge at Rye, which has been a useful feature in any case as trains regularly pass here. (Lens of Sutton)

51. This is the eastward scene, in October 1974. Gone are the gas lights, the crossover and the gates over Rope Walk but the crossing cottage and the Engineer's siding remained in 1986, a car and coach park having been constructed between the siding and the cattle market. (D. Cullum)

52. An open topped double deck bus was a good vantage point to enjoy the symmetry of William Tress' Italianate design. The parcels office on the right was tastefully added by the SR to replace a lean-to structure. Also impressive are the gateless gate pillars at the town end of the drive. (V. Mitchell)

APPLEDORE

53. Although the least elaborate of the original stations on the line, it was (and still is) a neat example of Tress' well balanced architecture. Unusually, the later canopy was added onto the side of the goods shed. The crude X on the print marks the position of the gentlemen's toilet, which was added in 1860. (Lens of Sutton)

54. An ex-LBSCR "Gladstone" class no. B184 drifts in from Ashford on 18th September 1929. As a junction station, it was unusual in not having a bay platform for terminating branch line trains. The signal on the left was therefore provided to start trains returning to New Romney from the up platform. (H.C. Casserley)

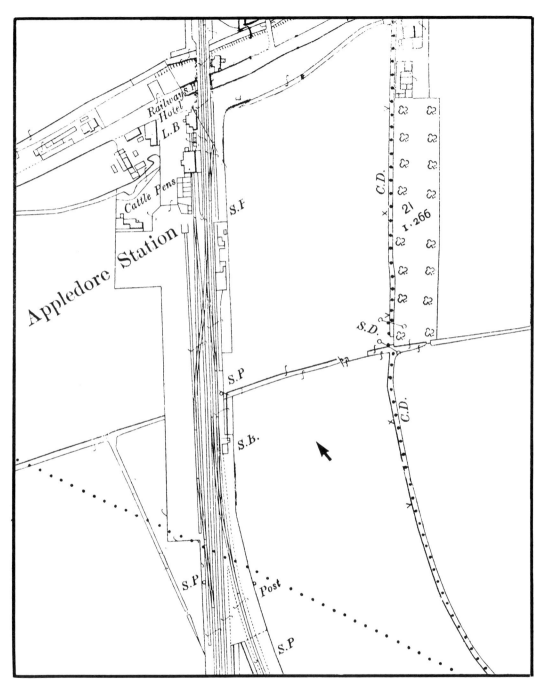

The 1907 map shows the original position
of the signal box (S.B.) which was replaced
by the present structure on 27th June 1954.

55. This and the next four pictures were taken in June 1958, to record different train movements. H class no. 31279 having run round its coaches in the goods yard, waits to form the 1.47pm all stations to Hastings. One of the straight sided DEMUs, built for the narrow tunnels on the Tunbridge Wells line, arrives at 1.41 from Hastings, probably on a driver training turn. (J.H. Aston)

56. The dummy signal nearest to us is "off", ready for class C no. 31589 to reverse off the up line. It has arrived, "light engine", to shunt the yard. The up starting signal was on a bracket to prevent it being obscured by the canopy. (J.H. Aston)

57. A well coaled H class 0–4–4T, no. 31319, waits with the 10.11 am departure for New Romney. The next train was at 10.54 and came through from Ashford. The lamp door is open and it contains a pressurised oil lamp, a vast improvement on the wick type. (J.H. Aston)

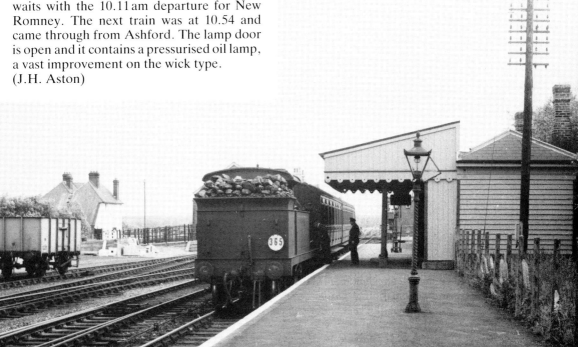

58. The signalman collects the Lydd single line tablet from the driver of H class no. 31522, which departed for Ashford at 9.58 am. Beyond the 37-lever signal box is a solitary goods siding, the others being on the up side. Only three semaphore signals remained in 1987 and the gates had been replaced by lights with no barriers. (J.H. Aston)

59. An eastbound train is propelled past the down platform, whilst empty stock stands at the end of the goods yard. The tender had been converted as a drinking water carrier by providing normal drawgear and a flexible discharge pipe, seen hooked up along the frame. Few of the 13 crossing keepers' houses on the branch had mains water supply – the crossings are now unstaffed and only the A259 crossing has automatic lights. (H.C. Casserley)

60. The single siding was removed and a footpath laid in its place so that the dangerous passenger crossing between the platforms could be eliminated. Photographed in 1967, all the buildings remained intact 20 years later, the goods shed being occupied by Paper Pots Ltd. (E. Wilmshurst)

61. A 1976 photograph shows the crossing keeper's cottage beyond the gates, the latter being wheel operated from the modern signal box. The previous box had been close to the junction (S.B. on the map). In 1987, only Rye and Appledore booking offices were manned and this charming crossing cottage remained in use as a dwelling. (J. Scrace)

THE NEW ROMNEY
BRANCH

62. As mentioned in the brief history at the front of this album, about two-thirds of the branch is retained for traffic from the nuclear power station. Despite the uniform flat scenery as seen here, the branch attracted four rail enthusiasts' specials in 1985, the year that it was on the approved list for such trains. Each had an extraordinary name – this is the "Dungeness Pebbledasher" behind no. 33201 on 13th April 1985. (J.S. Petley)

0063   0063

7   3   6   9   10   11   12

British Railways Board (S)

BROOKLAND HALT
PLATFORM TICKET 3d.

Available one hour on day of issue only.
Not valid in trains. Not transferable.
To be given up when leaving platform.
For conditions see over

1   2   3   4   5   6

3739   3739

SOUTHERN RAILWAY.

This ticket is issued subject to the By-laws,
Regulations and Conditions stated in the
Company's Time Tables, Bills and Notices.
Available on DAY of Issue ONLY.

Brookland Halt to

Brookland Halt   Brookland Halt
Ashford (Kent)   Ashford (Kent)

ASHFORD (KENT)

THIRD CLASS   THIRD CLASS
Fare 1/5   Fare 1/5

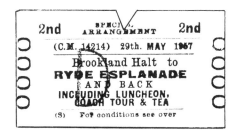

0000   0000

2nd   SPECIAL ARRANGEMENT   2nd

(C.M. 14214)   29th. MAY 1957

Brookland Halt to
RYDE ESPLANADE
AND BACK
INCLUDING LUNCHEON,
COACH TOUR & TEA

(S)   For conditions see over

BROOKLAND

63. This is the view towards Appledore, before the loop was removed in about 1920. The signal box was then removed and the station building eventually became a dwelling. (Lens of Sutton)

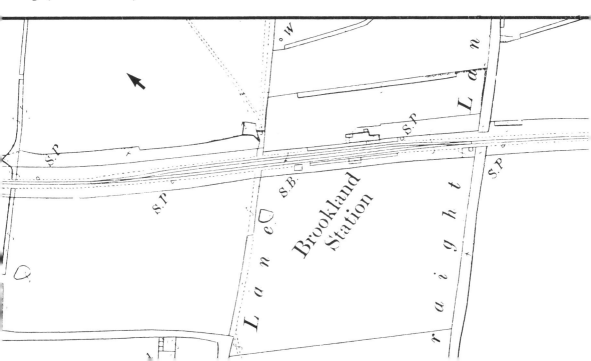

64. The lamp on the left was provided to illuminate the path to the road which was laid when the down platform was taken out of use. The train is the 12.47 pm from Ashford on 4th June 1958. (J.H. Aston)

65. It became designated a halt but was staffed by one man who acted as gate keeper, booking clerk and everything else. A small brick building with metal window frames was erected, alongside the road (A259) to accommodate him. (H.C. Casserley)

66. Whilst Appledore is over a mile from its station, the residents of Brookland and Brenzett had just under a mile to walk for a train. The advent of improved road transport made this a very quiet station, not even goods sidings were ever provided. (Lens of Sutton)

LYDD TOWN

67. The station received the suffix "Town" when the SR opened Lydd-on-Sea in 1937. It seems that the bracket for the signal was not really necessary, as it was replaced by a straight post later. (Lens of Sutton)

68. The Army established camps on the shingle wastes south and west of the town, prior to WWI. These generated a large amount of traffic on the branch, particularly after a railway was laid into the camp. (Lens of Sutton)

69. Not only did thousands of men have to be transported, but their horses also. Here we see the Wessex Territorial Royal Garrison Artillery unloading their steeds from *cattle* trucks, which have been heavily lime-washed as a disinfectant measure. (E. Carpenter collection)

The 1907 map shows the line to the army camp curving south from the goods yard.

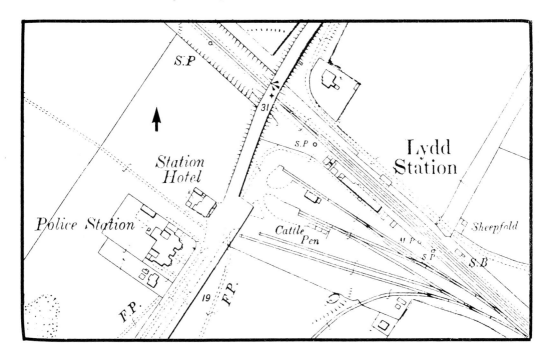

70. In this age of liquid fuel it is easy to forget the vast amount of fodder that was required to generate a few horsepower, particularly for an army. The picture at Rye also illustrates the point. Students of rolling stock should note that the wooden centred Mansell wheels, the long springs and the screw couplings suggest that this wagon had been built on a former passenger coach frame. (E. Carpenter collection)

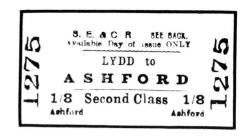

S. E. & C R   SEE BACK.
Available Day of issue ONLY

LYDD to
ASHFORD

1/8   Second Class   1/8
Ashford   Ashford

1275   1275

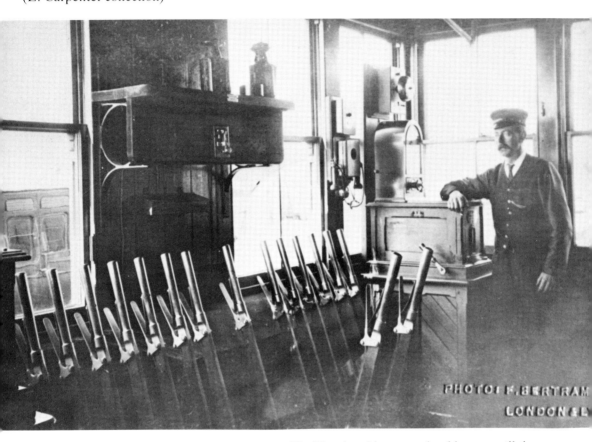

71. A print from a broken glass plate is worth including to show the extent of the staff at Lydd in Edwardian times. No. 8 was the last of a batch of railmotors built by Kitson & Co for the SECR and ran from 1906 until 1918. (E. Carpenter collection)

72. The signal box remained in use until the end of passenger services whereas the next box south of it, Romney Junction closed in 1911. Thereafter, the points were operated from a ground frame by the guard. The domestic style sash windows, favoured by the SER, are evident, as is Signalman Barham. (E. Carpenter collection)

73. This picture portrays the bleak feature-
less landscape south of Lydd which is composed of infertile shingle devoid of trees. The
iron shed housed the permanent way trolley –

hence the sleepers lying in the "four-foot".
There are at least five passengers and the
goods yard seems fairly full. (A.F.E. Field)

74. The 7th June 1958 and a summer gale blows the spare steam horizontally. Class 2 2–6–2T no. 84020 arrives with the 10.40 am from Ashford as class H 0–4–4T waits to leave with the 10.50 from New Romney. The iron shed seen here was the oil store. (J.H. Aston)

75. Class H no. 31263 stands by milepost 71¾ on 25th February 1962 and is now preserved on the Bluebell Railway. It is followed by no. 31690, one of the SECR C class, an example of which is also to be found on that line now. The railtour is signalled to run down to New Romney through the up platform. (S.C. Nash)

76. A 1967 view shows more clearly the lower signal arm which is a shunt signal for calling on trains, prior to reversal into the goods yard. Further south, a siding had been provided (on the east side) for coal traffic to the water works and one for the British Quarrying Co. on the west side. (E. Wilmshurst)

77. One of the other railtours of 1985 was the "Darkle Dungeness", on 28th July, and is seen with no. 33210 trailing, as it leaves for Dungeness. To the left of the roof, in the distance, is a gravel winning plant, while to the right, part of the two nuclear power stations is visible. The photograph is taken from the only overbridge on the branch and as this was not suitable for the power station construction traffic, the level crossing in the foreground was provided in 1961. (S.C. Nash)

78. The western facade remained unchanged in 1987, even retaining its small entrance canopy. In view of the importance of the station in a long chapter of the town's history, many will hope that the planning authority will ensure its survival. (V. Mitchell)

NEW COASTAL SERVICES.

Margate, Dover, Folkestone, Brighton, etc.

Week Days. / Sundays.

		a.m.	a.m.	a.m.	d a.m.	a.m.	a.m.	c p.m.	p.m.	p.m.	p.m.	p.m.	a.m.	b a.m.	
Margate Sands	dep.	6 55	....	....	8 10	....	9 25	....	2 45	....	....	4 5	8 35	....	....
Ramsgate Town	„	7 8	....	....	8 23	....	9 38	....	2 58	....	....	4 18	8 50	....	....
Sandwich	„	6 52	....	....	8 17	....	....	8 48	2 43	....	....	4 19	8 44	....	....
Deal	„	6 45	6S58	....	....	8 30	....	9 10	2 38	....	....	4 25	8 37	....	....
Walmer	„	....	7E3	....	....	8 35	....	9 15	2 33	....	....	4 30	....	8 30	....
Dover Priory	„	....	7E26	6S35	....	8 57	....	9 35	....	....	2J50	4 52	....	8 53	....
Dover Marine	„	....	7F34	....	....	9 3	....	9 45	....	2F50	....	4 58	....	9 5	....
Folkestone Central	„	....	7E55	6S59	....	9 21	....	10 7	....	3F8	3H8	5 18	9 16	9 23	....
Canterbury West	„	7 41	....	....	8 49	....	10 0	....	2 15	....	....	4 53	9 33	9 44	....
Ashford (Kent)	arr.	8 15	8E19	7S34	9 15	9 41	10 23	10 29	2 42	3F28	3H42	5 35 5 40			

			a.m.		9 50		11 0		4 7			6 21	9 50		
Ashford (Kent)	dep.		8 25		9 50		11 0		4 7			6 21	9 50		
Hastings	arr.		9 25		10 30		11 52		4 47			7 20	10 38		
Hastings	dep.		9 30		10 38		11 55		4 50			7 23	10 45		
St. Leonards (Warrior Square)	arr.		9 34		10 41		11 58		4 53			7 26	10 48		
St. Leonards (West Marina)	„		9 38		10 45		12 3		4 57			7 30	10 52		
Bexhill Central	arr.		9 46		10 53		12 11		5 5			7 37	10 59		
Eastbourne	arr.		10*15		11*22				5*33			8 2	11*31		
Eastbourne	dep.		8*48		11*0		12*15		5*10			....	11*0		
Lewes	arr.		10 36				12 45		5 39			....	11 32		
Brighton	„		10 32		11 48		1 2		6 0			....	11 50		
Brighton	dep.		....		noon 12 0		1 50		6 23						
Chichester	arr.		....		12 56		3 0		7 50						
Salisbury	„		....		2 35		....		....						
Exeter (Queen Street)	„		....		4 37		....		....						
Ilfracombe	„		....		6 54		....		....						
Bath	„		....		3 58		....		....						
Bristol (Stapleton Road)	„		....		4 22		....		....						
Newport	„		....		5 2		....		....						
Cardiff (General)	„		....		5 25		....		....						

Week Days. / Sundays.

		a.m.	a.m.	a p.m.	p.m.	d p.m.	p.m.	b p.m.	
Cardiff (General)	dep.	....	....	....	....	12 10	....	....	....
Newport	„	....	....	....	....	12 22	....	....	....
Bristol (Stapleton Road)	„	....	....	....	....	1 14	....	....	....
Bath	„	....	....	....	....	1 38	....	....	....
Ilfracombe	„	....	....	....	....	10J10	....	....	....
Exeter (Queen Street)	„	....	....	....	....	12K30	....	....	....
Salisbury	„	....	....	....	....	3 5	....	....	....
Chichester	„	....	8 44	....	3 2	4 41	....	....	....
Brighton	arr.	....	9 53	....	3 56	5 33	....	....	....
Brighton	dep.	7 35	10 15	1 12	4 10	5 55	6 19	5 45	....
Lewes	„	7 59	10 37	1 29	4 32	6 14	6 42	6 2	....
Eastbourne	arr.	8*43	11*23	2*7	5*19	6 35	7*21	6*36	....
Eastbourne	dep.	7*53	10*50	1*30	4*50	6 5	6*38	6*0	....
Bexhill Central	dep.	8 49	11 25	2 2	5 20	6 56	7 19	6 36	....
St. Leonards (West Marina)	„	8 57	11 32	2 9	5 27	7 5	7 28	6 42	....
St. Leonards (Warrior Square)	„	9 1	11 36	2 14	5 31	7 10	7 31	6 46	....
Hastings	arr.	9 5	11 40	2 18	5 35	7 14	7 35	6 50	....
Hastings	dep.	9 10	11 50	2 23	5 40	7 18	7 40	7 0	....
Ashford (Kent)	arr.	10 7	12 51	3 10	6 30	7 56	8 37	7 42	....

		a.m.	a.m.	a.m.	p.m.	p.m.	p.m.	p.m.	p.m.	p.m.	p.m.	p.m.	p.m.	p.m.	p.m.	p.m.	p.m.	p.m.
Ashford (Kent)	dep.	10 54	11 5	11 12	3 33	3 36	7E0	7 5	7S30	8 8	8 1	9S0	9 30	9 36	7 50	8 0		
Canterbury West	arr.	....	11 25	....	....	3 56	....	7 25	....	8 28	....	....	10 8			8 20		
Folkestone Central	„	11 11	....	....	3 50	....	7E20	....	8S5	....	8 18	9 23	10 1		8 10	....		
Dover Marine	„	11 27	....	....	....	....	....	....	8S25	....	8 35	....			8 27	....		
Dover Priory	„	....	....	11 59	4 17	....	....	....	....	8 49	....	10 23			....	....		
Walmer	„	....	....	12 17	4 25	....	....	8 9	....	9 6	....	10 44			....	9 7		
Deal	„	....	12 20	....	4 30	....	....	8 2	....	9 11	....	10 49			....	8 57		
Sandwich	„	....	12 12	....	5 40	....	....	7 51	....	9 12	....	....	10 48		....	8 48		
Ramsgate Town	„	11 53	....	....	....	4 22	....	7 58	....	8 56	....	....	10 44		....	8 46		
Margate Sands	„	12 5	....	....	....	4 31	....	8 10	....	9 8	....	....	10 58		....	9 0		

NOTES.

a Through Coaches Brighton to Ashford (Kent). b Through Coaches Dover Marine to Brighton, or *vice versa*.
c Through Coaches Margate to Brighton. d Through Coaches Folkestone to Brighton, or *vice versa*. E Except Saturdays.
F Mondays and Saturdays. H Except Mondays and Saturdays. J Leaves Ilfracombe at 10·50 mrn. on Saturdays.
K Leaves Exeter at 12·45 aft. on Saturdays. S Saturdays only. * Eastbourne passengers change at Polegate.

LYDD MILITARY RAILWAY

79. Construction of the camp started in 1883 and in 1885 the first two steam locomotives arrived – both Manning Wardle 0–6–0STs. The track layout changed from time to time and was up to six miles long. This view, from about 1890, shows some dual gauge track with Lydd church and windmill in the background. The latter burnt down in 1900.
(E. Carpenter collection)

Part of the extensive system in 1907.

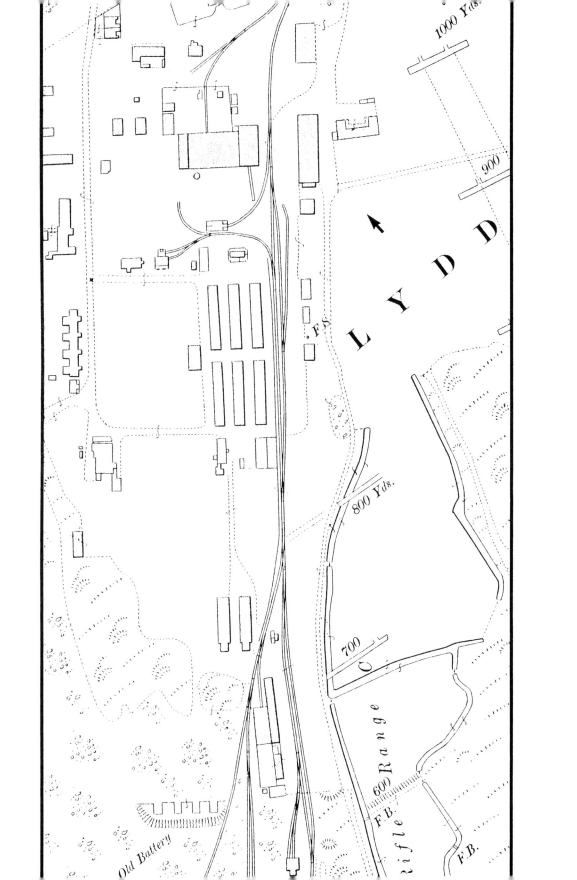

1000 Yds.

900

L Y D D

F.S.

800 Yds.

700

Range

600

Rifle

F.B.

F.B.

F.B.

Old Battery

80. Troops are seen unloading a 4.7 ins. gun in about 1912. The railway was largely lifted in 1926-27 but some 60 cm. gauge track remains in use today carrying mobile targets. (Lens of Sutton)

81. This is *Nicholson*, acquired new from John Fowler & Co in 1907. A new 0–6–0ST had been bought in 1906 from Hunslets and named *Napier*. Finally two 0–4–0STs were purchased in 1916-17. Only two passenger coaches were recorded on the system. (Lens of Sutton)

82. A train load of essential military equipment crossing the temporary timber roadway includes two traction engines, two conventional steam rollers and an unusual tandem roller introduced by Aveling and Barford in 1921. Its chimney and smokebox have been lifted off the vertical boiler and stood at its side, for the journey. (Lens of Sutton)

Dungeness
Coastguard Station
(Lloyd's Signal Station)

F.S.

The 1907 edition shows a siding running
north to a ballast pit. Many of the flints origi-
nated in cliffs at Beachy Head and were
destined for the Potteries of Staffordshire.
As late as 1979, ARC was transporting
shingle by rail to Ore.

W

Dungeness
Station

F.P.

19

F.P.

Lighthouse
(White, Revolving)

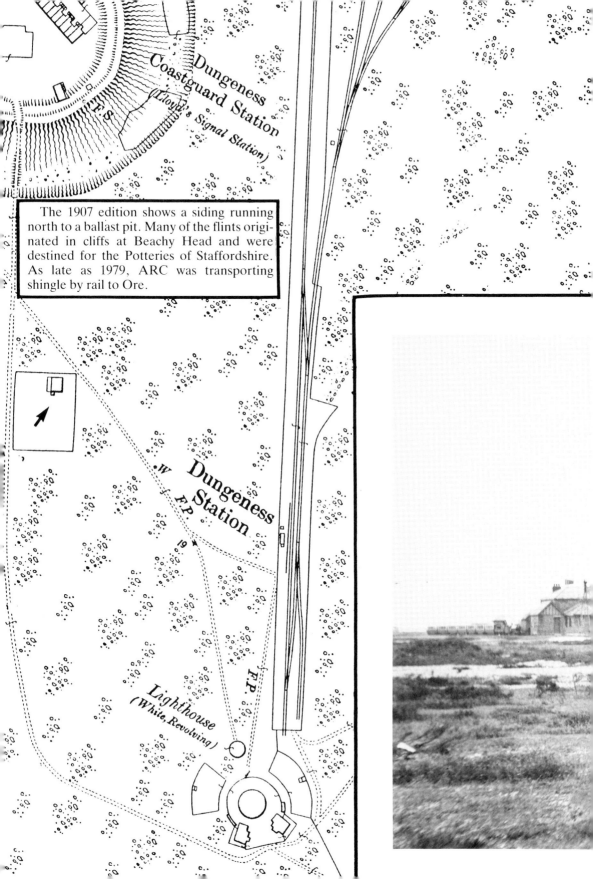

DUNGENESS

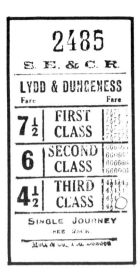

83. This southernmost point of Kent was not only the site of a lighthouse but also a coastguard station, a pilot station and an Admiralty signalling station were located there. On the left of this 1936 view, a RHDR 15″ gauge train stands at the terminus. (S.W. Baker)

84. Little vegetation is able to grow on the windswept acres of shingle – once described as "that part of the land that God forgot to finish". Class O1 no. A370 appears to be fresh from an overhaul, with its springs and hangers reflecting in the new paintwork. Maybe it is on a gentle running-in turn on the near-level branch on 5th September 1930. (Pamlin Prints)

85. Two years after closure in 1937, the tiny station was still intact although a small shed was added at one time as a ticket office, the station master from Lydd coming down on the train to man it. The "Admiralty Siding" passed through the gate on the left.
(R.F. Roberts)

86. About 150 yds of the New Romney branch and of the Dungeness line exists today, the latter including a run round loop. Flatrol wagons are loaded with steel flasks containing spent nuclear fuel rods for reprocessing at Sellafield in Cumbria. An impressive demonstration of the safety of this method of transport was given in 1984 when a driverless class 46 locomotive, with three coaches, was allowed to collide with an overturned flask, at 100 mph. The simulated rods were unscathed. Normally, one wagon a week is handled here on average but movements are unpredictable. (R. Wills)

LYDD-ON-SEA

87. The diversion of the New Romney branch nearer to the coast was intended to stimulate development of the area and a spacious island platform with double track was built. The anticipated crowds never arrived and the loop was lifted in 1954, having been seldom used. (Lens of Sutton)

88. The SR planned a substantial station but only this shed and a footbridge were erected. Stationmaster Sullivan watches a railwayman load his bicycle. This man and the photographer were the only passengers on the 3.01 pm from New Romney on 7th June 1958. (J.H. Aston)

GREATSTONE-ON-SEA

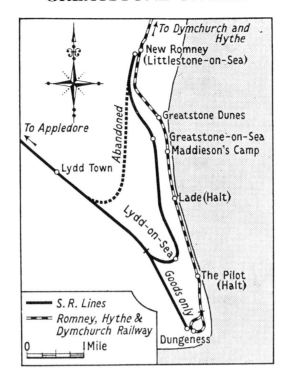

(Railway Magazine)

89. This was the other of the two stations opened in 1937. We look south, along the boundary of the shingle and Denge Marsh, towards the chalets of Maddieson's Holiday Camp, situated on the sea front. A single oil lamp has been attached to one of the functionless electric lamp-posts, as a gesture towards station lighting. (Lens of Sutton)

90. No permanent buildings were erected but a spacious concrete car park was laid out and remains to this day, outside Greatstone Primary School. BR standard class 2s were well suited to the branch – no. 84020 of that class returns from New Romney, with 1.00 pm departure on 7th June 1958.
(J.H. Aston)

91. Half a mile from the terminus, the new route (on the left) is shown joining the original one, on 3rd July 1937, the day before the change over. The lighthouse is visible in the distance, over four miles away. (R.F. Roberts)

92. Class R1 no. 31710 catches the evening sun on 13th May 1950 as it approaches New Romney. The line here returned onto useful pasture land, although any trees were deformed by the wind, as can be seen here. (S.C. Nash)

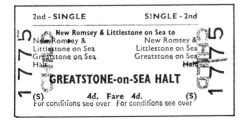

2nd - SINGLE — SINGLE - 2nd
New Romsey & Littlestone on Sea to
New Romsey &
Littlestone on Sea — Littlestone on Sea
Greatstone on Sea — Greatstone on Sea
Halt — Halt
GREATSTONE-on-SEA HALT
(S) — 4d. Fare 4d. — (S)
For conditions see over For conditions see over
1775

2nd - SINGLE
New Romney to
LYDD-on-SEA HALT
4d. FARE 4d.
FOR CONDITIONS SEE OVER
CHILD 0803

NEW ROMNEY

93. Sheep have for long been an important part of the economy of the area, Romney Marsh giving its name to a breed. Because of the severe winds and waterlogged ground, most of the flocks are moved miles inland in winter, giving the railway welcome extra traffic. This postcard view is believed to date from about 1915. (E. Carpenter collection)

94. This was the extent of the station staff around 1912. The advertisement reads TANGYE GAS & OIL ENGINES. These stationary engines were popular for water pumping and electricity generation before the advent of mains.
(E. Carpenter collection)

SOUTHERN RAILWAY.
Available DAY of Issue ONLY. (SEE BACK)
New Romney and
Littlestone - on - Sea TO
LONDON BRIDGE
Via Ashford or Hastings
9/3   Third Class   9/3
London Bridge   London Bridge

214

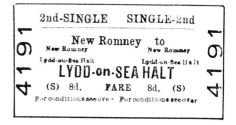

2nd-SINGLE   SINGLE-2nd
New Romney to
New Romney   New Romney
Lydd-on-Sea Halt   Lydd-on-Sea Halt
LYDD-on-SEA HALT
(S) 8d.   FARE   8d. (S)
For conditions see over · For conditions see over

4191

NEW ROMNEY & LITTLESTONE ON SEA

1907

Gas Works

New Romney & Littlestone on Sea Station

Allotment Gardens

S.P.

S.R.

S.P.

Goods Shed

Sta
He

95. Normally, only one platform was used by passengers although the 1907 map and photograph no. 93 show a waiting shelter on the up side. It was presumably the one authorised in 1901. Class B no. A458 awaits its headcode, circa 1927.
(S.C. Nash collection)

96. Ex-LCDR class R 0–4–4T stands in front of the parcels shed, neatly lined-out in Southern livery. The lush grass on the up platform was no doubt a bonus for the first batch of sheep to be loaded for their autumn journey. (Lens of Sutton)

97. Class D3 no. 32368 pulls a "Birdcage" set out of the goods yard prior to setting them back onto the two normal two-coach branch set. These extra coaches had conveyed a party to visit the RHDR in the morning and were being shunted for their return journey in the afternoon. (S.C. Nash)

98. A rare view of a mixed train (passengers and goods) on the branch. This economical method of working was permitted as far as Lydd, where the wagons had to be left for a goods train to collect. The RHDR to the left was originally double track throughout, but this was largely destroyed south of New Romney towards the end of WWII. This section was relaid as single track from the points on the far left. Whilst all the narrow gauge platforms are on the other side of the road, the northbound platform for trains from Dungeness was against the concrete wall, in 1928-29. (Lens of Sutton)

99. The SR offered a two-tier parcels service, similar to our present letter post system, but they were sent by goods or passenger trains, hence the need for a separate shed on the passenger platform. The level crossing gates at the end of the loop protected the siding to the RHDR. (D. Cullum collection)

100. The standard gauge siding is on the left of this 1959 view of the RHDR station. The train shed has subsequently been rebuilt across the site of the siding but one level crossing gatepost remains to indicate its position. (G. Barlow)

101. BR locomotives ventured onto the private siding to collect empty coal wagons but usually fly-shunted full ones from a distance. The brakes failed to function on one such wagon and it ran through the doors of the shed at the end of the line which housed the Duke of Sutherland's 0–4–4T *Dunrobin*. On the right are some tipper wagons and some open coaches, on their side. (G. Barlow)

102. The driver, the guard and two youngsters witness the coupling of the H class no. 31319 on 7th June 1958, whilst luggage is loaded into the van. The signal box once stood at the end of the grass-covered platform, as shown on the map. (J.H. Aston)

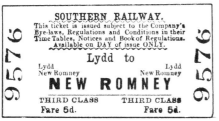

SOUTHERN RAILWAY.
This ticket is issued subject to the Company's
Bye-laws, Regulations and Conditions in their
Time Tables, Notices and Book of Regulations.
Available on DAY of issue ONLY.
Lydd to
Lydd   Lydd
New Romney   New Romney
NEW ROMNEY
THIRD CLASS   THIRD CLASS
Fare 5d.   Fare 5d.
9576   9576

103. The closure notice was the only poster to be seen on 25th February 1967, as a DEMU throbbed in the platform. The area now forms a neat and useful industrial estate. (E. Wilmshurst)

HAM STREET

104. At the end of the siding on the left is a wagon turntable which links with a track crossing the main lines under the engine. These features are shown on the 1907 map but the direct connection to the up yard is not, so this is presumably a later picture. Note the nameboard, remote from a platform, and the climbing roses. (Lens of Sutton)

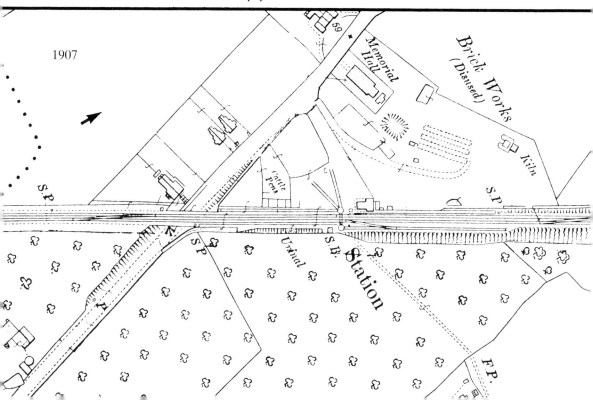

1907

105. Unlike most of the signal boxes we have seen on our journey, this one has the more common sliding windows. The lamp-post is of the barley sugar type and the lantern has the station name usefully incorporated in it. The suffix "Orlestone" was officially bestowed on 1st February 1897. (Lens of Sutton)

106. Three photographs from June 1958 illustrate this charming country station admirably. The signalling instruments are in profile as the ageing motor train passes wooden and steel examples of the 10-ton mineral wagon. A lady goes shopping while the porter prepares to hand an envelope to the guard. (J.H. Aston)

107. The same train, the 9.25 am from New Romney, pushes off to Ashford, the engine blowing off as it restarts up the 1 in 100 gradient. The noise partly obscures the crisp bark of the exhaust, which would have been music in the photographer's ears.
(J.H. Aston)

108. Looking down the hill towards the Marsh, it is evident that we have returned to the land of the trees – there are even orchards nearby – once a source of considerable rail traffic. (H.C. Casserley)

109. A 1982 view shows the attractive veran-
dah which was erected unusually on *three*
sides of the elegant building. It is worth looking at the differences and similarities to
Winchelsea station. (D. Cullum)

110. It is one of the few stations in the south
of England to retain a foot crossing for passengers but the nature of the timetable makes
it very safe. Large numbers of school pupils
use this station for their journey to Ashford.
(D. Cullum)

111. A mile south of Ham Street, Ware-horne Crossing takes a minor road over the line, close to where the latter crosses over the Royal Military Canal. This view from the south side in 1973 shows the enormous length of single gates which are braced by two long tie rods. This and the next crossing were fitted with automatic half barriers in 1981. (D. Cullum)

112. 1½ miles north of Ham Street, a public siding was provided on the up side of the line, close to Ruckinge Crossing. During WWII, the War Department laid an additional siding from it to accommodate one of the rail-mounted super heavy guns, capable of firing shells to the coast. Similar sidings were laid into Golden Wood, further north, and Holly-bush, to the south, where good natural camouflage was available. These gigantic guns were also stationed at Appledore and New Romney on specially reinforced sidings during parts of 1941-42. (D. Cullum)

ASHFORD

113. Looking north east from the signal box on 12th May 1891, we see the SER station, with the two bays that could be used by local trains to Hastings. Beyond this station, the London, Chatham and Dover Railway had its own terminus. This was closed to passengers on 1st January 1899 (not 1905, as often stated) after which the two companies were operated by a managing committee and the system became the SECR. (Lens of Sutton)

114. The SER established a locomotive works (partly visible) in 1847 which survived until 1962. Wagon production continued until 1981 after which only components were dealt with. The Hastings line curves away in front of the works, the tracks on the right being carriage sidings. (Lens of Sutton)

115. An ex-LBSCR class B2X, no. B204, stands in the up bay platform. This locomotive was formerly named *Telford* and ran nearly a million miles before being withdrawn in July 1929. (E.R. Lacey collection)

116. On the left, the River Stour passes under the railway close to D Box. On the right, the Canterbury line curves away at the top; the locomotive works is in the centre and the wagon works in the foreground. The Hastings line passes between them. (British Rail)

1907

Steam Saw Mills

Tank

Allotment
Gardens

S.P

S.B.

S.P

Cattle Pens

Weir

Pole
Bay

126

Pavilion

Football Ground

117. A steam paradise was created on 18th May 1957, as "West Country" class no. 34104 tears through with a boat train; class E1 4–4–0 no. 31497 waits to leave with a Canter-bury train and class H 0–4–4T no. 31295 blows off at the head of a New Romney service. (A.E. Bennett)

118. The two-coach set used on the New Romney service in September 1958 was inadequate for the 4.35 pm departure, on account of the number of school children using this train. An ex-LSWR Maunsell coach has been added behind ex-SECR H class tank no. 31520, which is seen crossing the River Stour bridge. (P. Hay)

119. Two more ex-LSWR coaches are to be seen forming this train from New Romney on 17th September 1958. Many of the H class tanks were fitted for push-pull working, this one displaying its additional equipment and connections for that purpose. (P. Hay)

120. With the advent of electrification of the Kent Coast main lines, the bay platforms were eliminated and converted into loops in 1962. Despite the Minister of Transport (ironically, Mr. Marsh) giving consent for the closure of the route in 1969, strong public pressure eventually had the desired effect.

The words above the female undergarment – "No more bloomers Marsh" – must have had some impact. Let us hope the next public demonstration will be to celebrate the electrification of this interesting and varied link-line in the national system.
(J.A.M. Vaughan)

MP Middleton Press

Easebourne Lane, Midhurst, West Sussex. GU29 9AZ Tel: 01730 813169 Fax: 01730 812601
... WRITE OR PHONE FOR OUR LATEST LIST ...

BRANCH LINES

Branch Line to Allhallows
Branch Lines to Alton
Branch Lines around Ascot
Branch Line to Ashburton
Branch Lines around Bodmin
Branch Line to Bude
Branch Lines around Canterbury
Branch Line to Cheddar
Branch Lines to East Grinstead
Branch Lines to Effingham Junction
Branch Line to Fairford
Branch Line to Hawkhurst
Branch Line to Hayling
Branch Lines to Horsham
Branch Line to Ilfracombe
Branch Line to Longmoor
Branch Line to Lyme Regis
Branch Line to Lynton
Branch Lines around Midhurst
Branch Line to Minehead
Branch Lines to Newport (IOW)
Branch Line to Padstow
Branch Lines around Plymouth
Branch Lines around Portmadoc 1923-46
Branch Lines around Porthmadog 1954-94
Branch Lines to Seaton & Sidmouth
Branch Line to Selsey
Branch Lines around Sheerness
Branch Line to Southwold
Branch Line to Swanage
Branch Line to Tenterden
Branch Lines to Torrington
Branch Lines to Tunbridge Wells
Branch Line to Upwell
Branch Lines around Wimborne
Branch Lines around Wisbech

SOUTH COAST RAILWAYS

Ashford to Dover
Brighton to Eastbourne
Chichester to Portsmouth
Dover to Ramsgate
Portsmouth to Southampton
Ryde to Ventnor
Worthing to Chichester

SOUTHERN MAIN LINES

Bromley South to Rochester
Charing Cross to Orpington
Crawley to Littlehampton
Dartford to Sittingbourne
East Croydon to Three Bridges
Epsom to Horsham
Exeter to Barnstaple
Exeter to Tavistock
Faversham to Dover
Hastings to Ashford
Haywards Heath to Seaford
London Bridge to East Croydon
Orpington to Tonbridge
Swanley to Ashford
Tavistock to Plymouth
Victoria to East Croydon
Waterloo to Woking
Waterloo to Windsor

Woking to Portsmouth
Woking to Southampton
Yeovil to Exeter

COUNTRY RAILWAY ROUTES

Andover to Southampton
Bournemouth to Evercreech Jn.
Burnham to Evercreech Junction
Croydon to East Grinstead
Fareham to Salisbury
Frome to Bristol
Guildford to Redhill
Porthmadog to Blaenau
Reading to Basingstoke
Reading to Guildford
Redhill to Ashford
Salisbury to Westbury
Strood to Paddock Wood
Taunton to Barnstaple
Wenford Bridge to Fowey
Westbury to Bath
Woking to Alton
Yeovil to Dorchester

GREAT RAILWAY ERAS

Ashford from Steam to Eurostar
Clapham Junction 50years of change
Festiniog in the Fifties
Festiniog in the Sixties
Isle of Wight Lines 50 years of change

LONDON SUBURBAN RAILWAYS

Caterham and Tattenham Corner
Clapham Jn. to Beckenham Jn.
Crystal Palace and Catford Loop
East London Line
Finsbury Park to Alexandra Palace
Holborn Viaduct to Lewisham
Lines around Wimbledon
London Bridge to Addiscombe
Mitcham Junction Lines
North London Line
South London Line
West Croydon to Epsom
West London Line
Willesden Junction to Richmond
Wimbledon to Epsom

STEAM PHOTOGRAPHERS

O.J.Morris's Southern Railways 1919-59

STEAMING THROUGH

Steaming through Cornwall
Steaming through East Sussex
Steaming through the Isle of Wight
Steaming through Kent
Steaming through West Hants
Steaming through West Sussex

TRAMWAY CLASSICS

Aldgate & Stepney Tramways
Barnet & Finchley Tramways
Bath Tramways
Bournemouth & Poole Tramways
Brighton's Tramways

Bristol's Tramways
Camberwell & W.Norwood Tramways
Croydon's Tramways
Clapham & Streatham Tramways
Dover's Tramways
East Ham & West Ham Tramways
Eltham & Woolwich Tramways
Embankment & Waterloo Tramways
Enfield & Wood Green Tramways
Exeter & Taunton Tramways
Gosport & Horndean Tramways
Greenwich & Dartford Tramways
Hampstead & Highgate Tramways
Hastings Tramways
Holborn & Finsbury Tramways
Ilford & Barking Tramways
Kingston & Wimbledon Tramways
Lewisham & Catford Tramways
Liverpool Tramways 1. Eastern Routes
Maidstone & Chatham Tramways
North Kent Tramways
Portsmouth's Tramways
Reading Tramways
Seaton & Eastbourne Tramways
Southampton Tramways
Southend-on-sea Tramways
Southwark & Deptford Tramways
Stamford Hill Tramways
Thanet's Tramways
Victoria & Lambeth Tramways
Walthamstow & Leyton Tramways
Waltham Cross & Edmonton Tramways
Wandsworth & Battersea Tramways

TROLLEYBUS CLASSICS

Bournemouth Trolleybuses
Croydon's Trolleybuses
Maidstone Trolleybuses
Reading Trolleybuses
Woolwich & Dartford Trolleybuses

WATERWAY ALBUMS

Kent and East Sussex Waterways
London's Lost Route to the Sea
London to Portsmouth Waterway
Surrey Waterways

MILITARY BOOKS

Battle over Sussex 1940
Blitz over Sussex 1941-42
Bombers over Sussex 1943-45
Bognor at War
Military Defence of West Sussex
Secret Sussex Resistance

OTHER BOOKS

Betwixt Petersfield & Midhurst
Brickmaking in Sussex
Garraway Father & Son
Index to all Stations
London Chatham & Dover Railway
South Eastern & Chatham Railways

SOUTHERN RAILWAY VIDEO

War on the Line